Shut Up

And

Do The Work

A written piece by Stephanie Synclair

You've always known you were placed on this earth for more. It's time for you to step into the shoes that you've always known, deep down, you were meant to wear. Here's to you beautiful beings who are here to change the world.

6 Shut Up and Do the Work

How to Use This Resource

You will soon find that this piece of work, this resource, is much more than a book. It is that, but it is also a workbook, a journaling prompt, a dialog starter and so much more.

I purposely wrote *Shut Up and Do the Work* as a piece meant to be experienced, not just read. This means that as you go through it, you'll notice certain questions are asked. Questions to get your mind flowing toward one of success as opposed to thoughts of failure and self-defeat. Questions that ask you to go deeper than you may have gone at this point, as it relates to business.

Take your time going through the work. Answer the questions, highlight items that stand out to you, and feel free to write in the book. This is the purpose of the book's format.

Introduction

"Your vision of where or who you want to be is the greatest asset you have."

I can't tell you how many men and women I speak to regularly on sales calls, while hosting training sessions and workshops, or when I step off the stage, who share with me all the things they want to accomplish. I'm told I motivate them; that they want to accomplish what I have and more. I see the excitement in their eyes. How much they want it—and then, they prefix it with "but." The word . . . but. What trails afterwards is almost guaranteed to be total and complete bull. It's also guaranteed the "but" has completely halted pursuit of the very goal these men and women claim to want to have achieved. When you add "but," everything preceding it becomes null and void. This is a major reason, I often advise my clients to allow a period to be the end.

As these people continue to share all the reasons they haven't accomplished their goals or how they might accomplish them, the light visibly drains from their eyes. At the core, even though they really want to accomplish big things, they truly believe that in some way, something stands between them and what they desire—some mountain or set of mountains they must first climb to reach their goal.

This truly saddens me because there is one thing I know for sure. There are no mountains. Seriously. I know you may be sitting at here thinking, "This woman is completely out of her mind. She doesn't know my situation. She doesn't see these mountains." And I get it. There will be challenges but nothing you can't overcome. That, I can guarantee. Nothing is un-overcome-able.

Unless you choose not to overcome them.

I prepared this piece of work for the person, the business owner, the entrepreneur or soon-to-be, who is ready to let go of limitations and excuses—ready to permanently remove the impediments in their lives called mountains. This work is for the person ready to Shut Up and Do the Work.

Is that you?

Who Am I, and Why Should You Listen to Me, Anyway?

14 Shut Up and Do the Work

I know somewhere in the back of your mind you may be wondering, "Who is this women telling me my mountains don't exist?" You may even be thinking, "She just doesn't understand." Or, like many, you may think, "She was probably born with a silver spoon in her mouth," or "Someone gave her money to get started, to catch her big break."

I must say . . . those are great assumptions that would make for a great story. One worthy of being called a fairytale.

You see, my story couldn't be more different. I was born into a single-parent household. My mother, a nurse, firmly believed that you should go to school, get good grades, get a good job and save your money. From the very beginning, none of those "goals" sat well with me. I didn't know why, but I knew my path would be a bit different.

From time to time, I'm asked if I'd always known that I'd be an entrepreneur. I actually had no clue. It never crossed my mind—at least, not at first. I didn't come from a family of entrepreneurs, and none of my childhood friends came from entrepreneurial families. Everyone was taught roughly the same thing: go to school, get good grades, get a job, save money, buy a home, have a family. Hey, it's the American dream, right?

Maybe I am not the American-dreaming type of girl because, even today, thinking about it makes me a bit nauseous. At the age of 16, I decided I was done with high school. Just like that. I truly hated going. I wanted to study the world. I wanted to study other cultures. During my sophomore and junior years in high school, I'd skip class to go to the library and read biographies and autobiographies of millionaires and billionaires. *This* is where I was first introduced to the entrepreneur. It seemed as if all the people making an impact financially were entrepreneurs. I wasn't quite sure what kind of entrepreneur or how I'd be one so, for a little while, it became something I'd tuck into the recesses of my mind. At that point in my 16-year-old life, my thoughts were far from what was being taught in school, so I decided to obtain my GED and go directly to college.

I am sure that somewhere in the back of my mother's mind, she was terrified. After all, hearing your only daughter say she is going to drop out of school has to be a parent's worst nightmare. My plan would take me completely outside of what she might have planned for me, but I felt it was my path.

Within 30 days of revealing my change of plans to my mother, I took the GED, scoring in the top 10 percent. Not bad for a girl who left after the first semester of junior year. Not bad for a girl who had skipped school as many days as possible during the second semester of 10th grade and the first semester of junior high. I then proceeded to follow through with my plan to go to school to obtain a degree in broadcast communications and history. At this point, I thought I'd become a well-known investigative journalist. I had grown up watching Oprah, seeing the impact she had on the world. A woman, from the south, who decided she wanted something bigger for herself. And I wanted something bigger as well. I knew I'd change lives, write books, speak on stage and make a huge impact on the world.

You know, it's funny, but looking back, I am today exactly where I desired to be. I guess we can take it a bit further, because there have been many accomplishments in my life that come as a shock—even to me. Accomplishments I, nor others, would have expected of a "drop out."

As planned, I did go on to work a bit as a journalist, but it didn't last because I wasn't able to use my own "voice," my own views. I eventually accepted that journalism wasn't the field for me. By chance, I ended up in sales and marketing, and I excelled. I had a natural sales ability and a skill for getting anything, literally, in front of the right market. I loved every moment of it. What I didn't love, was working for someone else. I concluded that I was in the same position I found myself as a journalist. The voice, the product, wasn't my own. I didn't have the space to create, to make the difference I truly desired. Once again, I'd placed myself in a place and space similar to where I'd been in high school and as a journalist. I wanted to walk away. I wanted to quit.

Society has a tendency to make us feel as though we are failures when the idea of quitting comes up. I truly feel that failure is staying somewhere longer than we should to appease others. I'd seen others remain complacent, complaining about their current situations, never to do anything about it because society tells us that we should fit into a neat little box with a bow on it. I'd attempted to do that, and it didn't feel good to me. And with that, I quit my corporate job.

Now, this may not seem like a huge deal, but what I had not done was prepare to quit. I didn't have a huge savings . . . well, I didn't have a savings at all and, most importantly, I didn't have a plan. But there was something in me—a burning desire—that forced me to quit. There was no choice. Three months later, once the money from my small retirement account dwindled, I was down to $21, and in the process of being evicted and having my car repossessed, all within a few days of each other.

Now, looking back, I laugh at this situation, because as painful as it felt at the time, it was all necessary. It helped me find my place, which helped me get to where I am today.

And where is that?

I now have a business that I love, helping entrepreneurs market their business effectively, attract ideal clients and close sales. A business, with a waiting list, that services thousands of entrepreneurs globally. One that has allowed me to travel with my son and a nanny for a full year through Europe and Asia, all while running my business virtually. One that has allowed me to have my radio show in, Chicago, the number three market in the United States, and to host live events worldwide. I've been featured on FOX Business, NBC, ABC, Huffington Post and many, many more podcasts and radio shows, highlighting million-dollar-earning entrepreneurs.

You see, this same girl who dropped out of school because she would rather spend time in the library studying the lives of successful entrepreneurs, became one herself.

So who am I to talk to you about this?

The perfect person.

Part I

Shut Up

Talk Really Is Cheap

Talk . . .

It's really overrated.

Think about it. How many people have you heard say, "I'm about to do XYZ," and years later, they are still talking about the same thing? Even during my working days, I disliked "talk." Everyone else talked about disliking their job and quitting to do their own thing. Most are still there today. But why is that? Why is it that most people "talk" about accomplishing, yet never do? Why is it that the majority of people in our society choose complacency?

I've asked myself this many times. I can't tell you that I have an answer worthy of a Pulitzer Prize; however, I can tell you that I believe many want it but don't truly believe it's for them. The thought of doing something different from the "normal" has scared them shitless, and they believe there are too many obstacles standing in their way.

I was born in the wrong town.

I live in the wrong city.

I'm not smart enough.

I'm not pretty enough.

I'm a single parent.

My husband or wife won't let me invest.

I don't have family support.

I don't have an investor.

I can't get a grant.

What if my friends and family reject me?

What if people call me stupid?

I don't know where to start.

What if it doesn't work?

What if it does work, and I'm not prepared?

The list can go on and on and on. I'm sure you get the point. You may even see a bit of yourself here. It becomes easier to talk about what you want to do, followed by the reasons you can't do them—at least, not now, which really equates to ever because it's more comfortable to stay where you are than to risk it all for what you truly want.

I am often asked if I think an entrepreneur is born or made. This is a difficult question, and I prefer to respond with, "I believe it takes a special person to handle the risk associated with being successful."

If you stop any millionaire or billionaire and ask them how often they risk it all, you'll likely hear "daily." Great reward comes with risk. To create a successful business—scratch that—a life you love, you must be willing to risk it all. Even if it means losing a few friends, who no longer accept you or your way of thinking. Even if it means being scared shitless that you've made a huge mistake. Even if it means risking being called stupid and foolish in the beginning. Hey, I was called them all.

I can't tell you how many times I've felt a great sense of fear. The successful aren't numb to fear. We feel it and move through it anyway. Someone has to—it's part of the reason the 1 percent are the 1 percent, and the 99 percent are the 99 percent.

A few years ago, I made a *huge* investment in my business. I'd just gotten to the place where I could breathe a bit in business. Successful by most standards—not successful enough to drop six figures plus for mentorship, or so I thought. I knew I wanted to Quantum Leap. I knew I wanted to touch more lives, make a greater impact and cross the million-dollar mark. So, I literally emptied my account . . . to zero. Now, if you've never been there, let me tell you firsthand, that is a scary situation. I woke up the next morning in a hot sweat. I didn't know if I'd lost my mind. Dealing with that type of fear is something not everyone has the nerve to do, but I did and, since then, my business has multiplied tenfold.

That wasn't the first time I'd experienced such fear. I take huge risks regularly. Putting myself on the line is why I've been able to achieve so much. It's not that I love risk, but I do welcome it. I've never taken a risk that I've regretted. Ever.

Through the years of studying other successful entrepreneurs and building relationships with many, I am sure they will all tell you the same. There are some risks that put their stomach in knots. But either you take the risk or stay where you are.

The kind of risk where everything is on the line, many aren't willing to take. So, talking about it is easier. It makes for great conversation—but you'll get no reward.

An old saying goes, "Don't talk about it, be about it." Do you remember that? As a kid, I'd hear others say this to pressure other kids into doing something. As silly as it sounded at the time, it's one you may want to consider adopting, if success in business is something you truly desire.

5 Categories of Failure

During my years speaking and helping entrepreneurs build their businesses, I've discovered that although we are individuals, we all fall into certain categories. It doesn't matter how unique or different we are. It doesn't matter if our hair is purple, pink or green, how many tattoos we have or how spiritual we are. Overall, we are more alike than different and can be grouped into particular categories of thought.

A few years ago, I began to notice a few commonalities in those I'd meet who were the "talkers." At a glance, I could group them and tell you the likelihood of success.

This ability is something we all have if we pay attention and are present during conversations. Key words are used or not used. A clear thought process that can't be hidden, even if you're talking about the weather. You, too, will start picking up on it once you understand the 5 Categories of Failure: what each one looks like, feels like and sounds like. With this understanding comes the veil being lifted off your eyes and your ears being opened more. You'll find yourself listening to your innermost thoughts and realizing that you may be in one of these groups. If that happens, I don't want you to get angry with yourself. Realization is the first step to making a change.

Think about it. If you aren't aware of a problem, how can you fix it? If you have a drinking problem, until you realize it's a "problem," nothing tells you to fix it. Until you realize you've put on a little weight, nothing tells you to release it. Until you realize you're living in poverty, nothing tells you there's more to life.

Within the next few pages, I am going to share with you each of the five categories of failure. Some, you may have heard about; others, may never have crossed your mind—but you will clearly see how each one can set you up for failure.

The Dreamer

We have all met The Dreamer. This person embodies what defines a talker. Their days are spent dreaming about what they'd like to do, the perfect man or woman, the perfect job or business, a vacation they'd like to take. With them, the dreaming never stops.

Let me be clear about something. Listening to The Dreamer feels good. The Dreamer speaks to the part of us that desires more and knows we can have more. There is definite inspiration there. Because of this, The Dreamer has the ability to build a large following with people hanging on to every word. But that is where it stops.

We've all seen it.

A social media page with hundreds of thousands of followers, but it's not monetized.

A YouTuber with hundreds of thousands of views and subscribers who is still working a day job, unable to turn followers into finances, although, they may express a desire to do so.

The Dreamer doesn't have to be on a large-scale level.

It can be that person with a lot of friends. The "popular" one. This person talks a good game, but their life isn't changing.

Or maybe they don't have a following. Maybe they spend their days thinking about what they'd like to do, have, become and see. Maybe they've been wondering why they feel stuck, like there is a "block" of some kind.

A certain energy comes with being a dreamer. One such energy is their ability to build a following. This comes naturally for many of them. Unfortunately, this is usually where it stops, because dreamers have a tendency to spend more time dreaming than accomplishing.

I'm going to ask you a hard question. Is this you? How does it feel to hear yourself described in this manner? Do you get angry? Do you feel enlightened? Or do you feel you're ready to move from being a dreamer to an all-out doer?

The Lurker

I remember the first time I heard the term "lurker." The year was 2010, and I'd just started my YouTube channel. My page statistics showed hundreds of views, but no one commented or "liked" the videos. These silent visitors would come back time and time again but would rather watch than participate.

The Lurker sits back and watches what others do. They never comment, never participate and certainly never take action. Often, The Lurker is waiting for the "perfect time" or a "sign" that it's time to come out of hiding. But neither appears. So, the lurker spends their life, looking and lurking, wishing and wanting.

The Lurker may have a bit of "dreamer" inside of them, usually not discussing it outwardly. They'd rather watch others live "their dream" and wonder how they can as well.

Often The Lurker plans out the actions that must be taken, but never actually takes the action. This can happen on multiple occasions, with each time being "the time" they'll take action; however, nothing ever happens.

Do you see yourself in The Lurker? How does it feel to hear yourself described in this manner? Do you get angry? Do you feel enlightened? Or do you feel you're ready to move from being a lurker to an all-out doer?

The Hater

The infamous hater. We all know this person. Deep down, this one feels anger toward the success of others. The Hater will desperately hunt through the successes of others searching for evidence of failure. This is usually not a conscious act. If you were to confront them, they'll usually deny the hate and call it "truth."

A good person at heart, they've simply been bit by the envy bug.

The Hater attempts over and over to create success but is unable to grab hold of the reins. They are unsure as to why they seem to fall short, while others are apparently able to achieve success with seeming ease. When they see others reaching goals, they feel that the other person isn't deserving. On some level, they feel "hard work" is the key to success, but the harder The Hater works, the more they seem to fail. There is a deep sense of pain, because The Hater knows they are meant for more and feels as though they've been dealt a bad hand. Not quite realizing they shuffled the cards and dealt the hand.

Unable to be happy for the success of others, they'll never find success of their own.

The Hater is a category that it is easy to see in others and most difficult to see in ourselves. It requires deep reflection and honesty. It requires us to come out of victim mentality and step into our powerful selves. A "self" able to look in the mirror and see core truths, no matter how painful these truths may be. Such reflection is painful, because we are used to everyone outside of us being The Hater—not us.

Are you ready for truth? Are you ready to get completely naked and honest with yourself? Are you The Hater? Do you have hater tendencies? Do you struggle being happy for others, even strangers? Even those you dislike?

Now, truly embracing this without judgment, how does it feel to finally see yourself in this manner? Does it make you angry? What are the emotions that come up for you? Do you feel enlightened? Do you feel you're ready to move from being a hater to being truly happy for the success of others?

The Pessimist

If I give you a glass and fill it to the halfway mark, is it half full or is it half empty?

Seriously, close your eyes and imagine me pouring it. Which would you choose? Half full or half empty?

The Pessimist would certainly choose half empty. Everything in their lives is half empty. This pessimism may not have been conscious and probably isn't, but it's there all the same.

You may have had goals, large or small, and didn't move forward because "it probably won't work out anyway." You know right off that things aren't going to work out well for you. You want it to work, but history has shown you otherwise, so why even try?

Not trying seems easier than trying, to only fail. So, The Pessimist doesn't try.

And in those rare moments they do and don't succeed, a familiar voice says, "I told you so"; "You shouldn't have tried"; or "I knew this would happen. Due to this history of failures or perceived failures, when inspiration hits or opportunities arise, often The Pessimist will sabotage them to avoid failure.

For The Pessimist, it's better to have not tried than to try and fail.

Do you ever feel this? Have you ever felt this? What are some things you'd like to do or accomplish but fear of failing stopped you?

Here is the hard question. Are you ready to let go of the pessimism and take hold of optimism?

The Judge

Because you judge others, you're fearful others are going to judge you. The amount of success you'll ever obtain is limited because what others think weighs on you more than what you think about you. Then again, you are the harshest judge of yourself. But instead of judging against what you truly desire, you judge against what society says is right or wrong.

Judge not, lest ye be judged.

It's a scripture I heard quoted many times growing up. The older I get, the more I wonder if these scriptures and sayings are quoted without having properly interpreted the meaning or having absorbed the actual meaning. Despite hearing this scripture so repeatedly quoted, I grew up in a world where everyone judged. Behind the walls and around the dinner tables, the lady down the street or around the corner was being discussed as well as the lady who attended church who slept with so and so.

I grew up knowing I wasn't to do certain things or behave a certain way, because I didn't want people to talk about me. I was brought up to do what is considered proper by society, so I wouldn't be judged. I worked hard to uphold that standard but, in the end, failed horribly. At least, according to those doing the judging. The moment I thought of dropping out of high school, I opened the door to be judged—by my school peers, my parents' circle and even today in business. The idea that a woman who has dropped out of everything from school to jobs now teaches women how to build financially successful businesses seems absolutely ludicrous to many people. There are a certain group of people who wouldn't touch my reality with a ten-foot pole. But when I stopped judging myself, what others thought of me no longer mattered.

The Judge is failure 5. I left this for last, as it is the one that the majority struggle with. We unconsciously judge everyone and everything. Even for me, being nonjudgmental is something I must consciously practice daily. This is a behavior that has been ingrained in us. When others don't look the way we expect or act the way we expect, when they say something that doesn't seem fitting or dress in a way that isn't the societal norm, naturally, we tend to judge.

With the tendency to judge others, comes the fear that others will judge us. I know a lady who often thinks others are judging her. She tries to live the "perfect" life. Remember these lyrics by Carly Simon, "You're so vain, you probably think this song is about you"? These words describe her perfectly, except hers isn't about her being vain. Because she spends her life judging the actions of others, she constantly thinks others are judging her as well. When this initially came to my attention, I found it a bit funny. I mean, seriously, do you think everyone is talking about you? That is, until I realized that every time she speaks, she's in judgment of others. And because other people are a reflection of us, of course, she would think that others would judge her. She judges them.

I've run across many people who buy small business programs, products and services, only to get them and tear them apart. They judge them harshly, with only minimal good to say about them. I decided long ago that even if a service wasn't what I expected, I'd find all the good in it there was to be found. This has made my buying experiences amazing, and I tend to attract clients and customers of the same mindset. I rarely have someone "judging" me or my services. And if I do, I don't know it, because I am too busy building up others and what they have to offer.

Now, here is the hard question. Have you appointed yourself judge? Do you judge the lives and businesses of others? Do you pick apart every program or system you buy? Are you picking apart this piece of work right now? What are the things that are going through your mind as you read these words? Are you ready to admit that you fit The Judge? And are you ready to let go of judging so that you can release your greatness into the world without fear of being judged?

Maybe You aren't Meant to be Successful.

46 Shut Up and Do the Work

Contrary to what others will tell you, I don't believe everyone was meant to be financially successful. I know this may not be a "popular" opinion, but it certainly is true. If everyone were meant for it, everyone would be. The fact is, most aren't. Most will remain in their category of failure and never do more. You may be reading this at the moment, and you may be the one who is going to put this book down, because you don't feel you have what it takes to reach your goals. And if that is you, that is totally okay. Again, the one percent is the one percent for a reason. No harm, no foul in falling into the 99 percent.

Society has a tendency to put immense pressure on us. *Lifestyles of the Rich and Famous* (does this still air?), *Billion Dollar Buyer*, *The Fabulous Lifestyles of . . .* are just a few of the television shows that highlight the rich and famous. Then there's social media. With niche celebs popping up around every corner, private planes, yachts, Las Vegas penthouses, mansions, Rolls Royce's, Bentley's and Lamborghini's appearing on our social media timelines day in and day out, the pressure to create massive success is huge.

I am going to let you off the hook here and tell you something that many others won't have the balls (or ovaries) to tell you . . .

It is one hundred percent okay, if you truly don't want those things. Massive success is available for everyone but is not meant for everyone. Those are two completely different conversations. If success is something that doesn't call to you, that is completely okay, but be honest about it. Don't attempt to live up to the standards that others impose on you. Don't attempt to keep up with the Joneses. That shit will keep you unhappy, and what is the point of massive financial success if you're miserable?

I am sure you've heard the saying, "Money doesn't buy happiness." This usually occurs when the person is too busy living to please others and not themselves. If you can fully live to please you *and* stack your paper, do so! If not, choose happiness first, not money.

If you realize that success, not just financial, may not be for you—if you realize that you want to hold on to one of those 5-failure characteristics, then by all means do so. The rest of this piece of work is for the person who is ready to cut the excuses, has already committed to shutting up and is ready NOW to do the work necessary to reach their goals.

Part II

Do the Work

The Good News

Right now, you may feel a bit distraught. You've discovered what category or set of categories you fall into. The sheer fact you are still reading this tells me that although you've discovered this, you are ready for soul-stirring transformation. It tells me that you know deep down that right now, at this exact moment in your life, you are meant to do more and have more, you are meant to touch more lives than ever before, and you're ready to get out there, be visible and make a huge impact on the world. I am thrilled you are still here. I didn't scare you off!

I have good news for you! You weren't born into one of the five categories I listed!!! Right now, at the thought of that, you should be thrilled, because that means you can change your current conditioning.

Each of the five categories—The Dreamer, The Lurker, The Hater, The Pessimist and The Judge—are all taught traits. You weren't born just to dream. You weren't born to simply sit around and watch others do, be and accomplish. You were born as love, knowing within your cells that anything you desired is yours, and you certainly weren't born a judgmental being. Where true love lies, judgment cannot and will not live. Think about this for a moment. We are born as infants, and we are pure bundles of love. Everything we do, down to eating, is dictated by someone else. We are sponges soaking up everything around us, which means, at some point, we picked up the learned behaviors and thought patterns that tell us we aren't enough, that external environment dictates our future, that those who succeed "must be cheating," that we must conform to societal ways of thinking and being, that there is a "right and wrong" way to be, that money doesn't come easy, and that the likelihood of success isn't likely. These thought patterns and beliefs don't only come from our parents but our circle of friends as we are growing up.

When I think back on my life, I have to tell you that to the "normal" person, dropping out of school at sixteen and knowing I'd be accepted into college and have a successful career wouldn't be the thought they'd have. As a matter of fact, more people told me that I was making a mistake than pushed me to move forward. I actually had zero support. Now, I want to give my mother credit here because she had to sign the papers that allowed me to take my GED, but that was almost a "no choice" situation. I was determined to not go back to school. She could drop me off, and I would leave. She was frustrated with me, and I was frustrated with school. Signing those forms, and on some level trusting that I'd follow through with my plan, was the only option outside of me leaving school and not doing shit with myself. She had to trust my plan, even if she didn't want to. So if I had to pick anyone that "sort of supported me," I would certainly say my mother—just know it was disgruntled support.

I had no idea that the plan I'd created didn't make logical sense. In my 16-year-old mind that had been told ever since I could remember that I can do whatever and have whatever I desire, the plan was foolproof. I am often asked why I think that I am one of the few to leave school, immediately get a GED and follow that directly with college, and my answer is simple—I didn't know I couldn't. Because I truly thought anything was possible, every door I knocked on, opened. I had no problem getting into college, and I had no problem getting amazing positions at companies that many tried for years to work for. I didn't know I was supposed to struggle. I truly thought that every door I knocked on was meant to be opened.

Later in life, I began to acquire a new circle of friends. People who lived a different life from me, with different upbringings and experiences. I'd share my thoughts and dreams with them because that's what friends do, right? Now, at this moment, I was a dreamer that followed my dreams with massive action. A dream is only a failure if it remains a dream. I remember describing in detail where I desired my career to go, and I remember the exact day when I adopted a new truth, when I realized that I live in a dream world and "people like me don't achieve success." I was sitting in my friend's living room drawing out this picture. I explained how I was going to be a well-known television personality. I'd write multiple books that would go on to become best sellers, speak on stage in front of thousands and travel the world whenever I desired. I distinctly remember her blank stare, and when I was done, the laughter that filled the room. Once the laughter died down, she began to ask me how many people I knew who had come from meager beginnings and created success like that. She asked me how many women of color I knew from the Deep South, who were traveling internationally, speaking on stages and well-known personalities.

I told her the few I knew of, one being Condoleezza Rice, from Birmingham, Alabama, but not many outside of her. Now, a quick side note here is that I'd never even thought of others who had accomplished what I desired. It never occurred to me to do so. Having grown up in a multicultural community, it never occurred to me that something like my skin color or where I'm from would hold me back. Considering I grew up in the south, this might be shocking to most, but that simply wasn't my story.

My friend informed me that the reason I didn't see it was because I lived in a bubble and how big of a fool I was for believing that I could do more, have more and be more. I didn't believe her on a conscious level, but the seed was planted and, from that moment, and for years to come, I'd doubt myself and my abilities. This doubt showed up in small ways for me but made a huge impact. The girl who knew she could accomplish anything began to wonder if what my friend said were limitations would hold me back from positions. I began to notice that it wasn't as easy as it was previously to walk into a location, have a couple of interviews, send a letter and be hired. I began to be passed over more. And the words she told me began to seem true. You see, these learned behaviors and thought patterns come from everywhere, which is why it is so important to watch your surroundings. If you aren't being filled with life, you're being filled with death. There is no in between. Someone else's truth doesn't have to become your truth. It's their truth because they chose for it to be.

For years, my truth was that everything I touched turned to gold. In a time before I knew what an affirmation was, before I knew there was a "self-help" industry, I was speaking life because that is all I knew. But when I allowed someone into my world who spoke words other than life, who planted a seed in fertile ground, then my truth began to change. This is why it is not only important to filter what we hear and see, but also protect our children, to a degree, from what is seen and heard. Today, in the world of the Internet, this is much harder, but we are all they have, so we must do our best. You see, wherever you find life, positive thoughts, success mentality, you find fertile ground. Think about a garden. If the dirt isn't good dirt and the ground isn't fertile, you can plant seeds all day. Nothing will grow. But with fertile ground, everything you plant will grow. And for me, a seed was planted and proof was growing. It wasn't until I realized the correlation that I was able to get rid of the tree of doubt and failure that had grown and was producing someone else's fruit, and replace it with seeds that I wanted to grow.

This means that where you are right now, no matter what category you fall into, is all learned and can be unlearned. Think of it like a computer that has a virus. It has to be wiped clean, and then new software and systems uploaded. That's exactly what must happen for you to change your circumstances, situation and thoughts around success and what's possible. We need a complete wipe of our hard drive, so we can replace the information with the thoughts and patterns we desire.

80/20 Rule of Success

60 Shut Up and Do the Work

I love seeing the excitement on the face of new business owners. To sit down with them and listen to them speak, you can literally feel the energy bouncing off of them. They share how excited they are to work with me and how they can't wait to create their marketing strategy. Usually, thirty minutes are filled with all they want to do around marketing and lead generation, getting as much media and press as possible, and the world finding out about their amazing offerings. I am really excited for them. I know the feeling. But one thing I never hear mentioned, is the work they are going to do on themselves; the mindset work that that will be critical to achieving their goals.

Mindset work is a key piece many miss and, when you later dig in, you discover that many of the businesses that fail missed the fact that there is an 80/20 rule of success. Years before I became an entrepreneur, I studied the wealthy. I was curious about what it took to get there and stay there. I enjoyed listening to the stories of how massive wealth was built from virtually nothing. Since I've taken the steps to build my own successful business, I've been privileged to have met other successful entrepreneurs doing big things in their industries. I've had the opportunity to sit down and have probing conversations about the key shifts that took place in order for them to create the success they've achieved in their business. Even today, I watch interviews, listen to audios and read books about entrepreneurs who have created mega success. And do you know what the common denominator is from all of those? The one thing that everyone has in common is the way they think. They all spend massive amounts of time on different forms of mindset work. I quickly found out that only 20 percent of success is the actual action we take. A huge 80 percent of success is our mindset.

This is extremely important to note because more people are teaching the "hustle" and "grind" methods and not talking much about the other methods. This is a major reason why you meet so many people who talk about hustle and grind, yet aren't getting the results they want. It simply isn't enough.

Now, I do think it is worth noting that saying action is only 20 percent doesn't mean sitting around all day doing nothing. It means that in addition to massive actions you're taking, you must spend even more time on your mindset. Reprogramming and retraining your mind to that of the success you desire to be is imperative. If you're still thinking like the employee, you're going to find it difficult to create success. If you are still thinking like a pauper, you'll never be a prince.

Right now, you may be rolling your eyes into the back of your head thinking, "This lady is off-the-boat crazy." I get it. I follow an entrepreneur who I absolutely love. He pushes hustle day and night. With hundreds of thousands of fans, all of whom are hustling it out, you'd think there would be more success from those who follow him. But recently, in an interview I saw with him, the interviewees took a bit of a different approach asking him about the mindset behind his success. Turns out, he consciously works on it. Day in and day out, taking time to work on his mindset.

You see, no matter where you are, there is an upper limit and no amount of action can break that as upper limits are created internally.

Are you ready to break through your upper limit?

The 80 Percent

"A divided mind is one that will never accomplish what it truly desires because it knows not what it desires."

I am sure you are a bit tired of me saying it, but I can't put enough emphasis on it. Hustle and grind alone will not create the success you desire. The "action" is only a small percentage of what it takes to succeed, financially or otherwise. Eighty percent of success is your mindset. However, I don't want you to think that mindset isn't work or action. Often, mindset work is much more effort than the "action" you're used to taking when it comes to your business.

One of the hardest things I've ever had to do is reprogram my mind from one of lack to one of abundance. To go from thinking like the salaried employee of someone else's company, to thinking like an entrepreneur and CEO of my own company. Many ask why it is so difficult to let go of old mindsets and belief systems, but if you think about it, you didn't create this life you live, your thought process, and your beliefs, overnight—and you won't be able to get rid of them overnight. But with daily action, you will quickly see a difference. First, you'll start recognizing the thoughts that are keeping you from your desired outcome. Once you recognize the problem, you'll be able to replace it with statements that match the outcome you do desire.

The first key to creating the world you desire is to decide

exactly what it is you want. You must be specific. Now, this seems simple enough, but I can't tell you how many people I've run into who can't quite pinpoint what it is that they want to accomplish. One day they want to do X and the next day Y. A divided mind is one that will never accomplish what it truly desires because it knows not what it desires. So, you must first become crystal clear on what it is you desire in life.

Use the space below to write down specifically what it is you desire to accomplish and do, as it relates to life and/or business. Be as specific as possible. Let's make this super simple. What is it, specifically, you'd like to work on and accomplish over the next 12 months?

_____

_____

_____

_____

_____

_____

_____

_____

What is it you want to accomplish overall? When you die and people think of the work you were known for, what will they say?

_____

_____

_____

_____

_____

_____

_____

_____

The next step is to get clear on what you truly believe about accomplishing the things you said you want to accomplish. Let me give you an example: When I started my first business, my big desire was to make a million dollars for the year. When I sat down and began to do the work around creating the million, I realized I had beliefs around it that weren't serving that desire. For instance, I thought it would take me 5-plus years to cross the million-dollar mark. I also thought I'd have to have thousands of clients at once and a large staff to handle that number of clients.

Although that *could* be true, those thoughts weren't creating ease around the million dollars for me. They were actually doing quite the opposite. The more I thought about it, the further away the million-dollar mark seemed. I began to worry about how I'd ever get that many clients, if I didn't have a team in place and how I'd get a team in place, if I didn't have the clients and revenue to pay them. I remember in previous years someone asking me why I'd want to create a million-dollar-plus company anyway. They said that I was being greedy. Somehow, I began to think that I should be okay with less and maybe the reason I didn't feel great about what it took to create it was because I was only being greedy. A vicious cycle was created that in no way supported what I truly desired to establish. I encourage you to dig deep and think about the thoughts you have around what you desire. What are the beliefs that you hold around your goals and what it will take to accomplish them that do not truly support what you want?

Use the space below to write what comes up for you.

_____

_____

_____

_____

_____

_____

_____

_____

_____

I want you to know you have the ability to change your beliefs and thoughts. I remember years ago, when I first started following the work of Abraham Hicks and I heard, "A belief is simply a thought you keep thinking over and over until it becomes truth." I have to tell you that it sounded crazy as hell when I first heard it, but the more I thought about it, meditated on it and dug into the meaning, I began to realize its truth. The only reason I believed it would take me 5-plus years to generate a million plus dollars in my business, is because I heard someone say that's how long it took them. As I thought on it, it made total and complete sense to me, and that thought turned into a belief. So, of course, it made sense that if I could think a thought long enough to become a belief that did not serve me, surely, I could think a thought long enough for it to become a belief that did serve me. At that moment, the little light bulb you see in cartoons over the character's head, went off in my mind. The message I received was that *any* belief could be eradicated and replaced with one that served me, my purpose and where I desired to go.

To be sure, I performed a series of tests. I first tested my method on the limiting beliefs as it regarded the time it would take to reach a million, and then on the number of people I'd have to work with to reach it. Next, I tested it on the big team I thought I needed. I tested it out on my clients as well and quickly realized that this method does work on anything and everything you decide to use it on. Now, there are a few things that will slow up your progress, and I will share those with you in just a bit.

Let's start changing those beliefs.

I want you to think about each of the beliefs you previously listed that didn't serve you and what you fully desire. If that isn't your truth, what *is* your truth? In the space below, write the new statement that you are adopting as your truth.

Here is an example:

Original belief: I will need to work with thousands of people at low prices to create a million-dollar business.

New belief: I can create a million-dollar business working with a small number of people, who are excited about their growth and willing to pay me my worth.

Original belief:

_____

_____

New belief:

_____

_____

Original belief:

_____

_____

New belief:

_____

_____

Original belief:

_____

_____

New belief:

_____

_____

Original belief:

_____

_____

New belief:

_____

_____

Now say *out loud* the following statement:

"The belief that [insert original belief] is a lie. Other people may choose to allow that to be their truth, but my truth is [insert new belief]."

It is imperative you speak the statement out loud. The seed from that previous thought was likely planted verbally by someone at some point. So, verbally, make it known that it isn't true.

Also important, is to go back to the original statement, "A belief is simply a thought you keep thinking over and over, until it becomes truth." This means that until consciously and subconsciously you adopt this as your truth, you must consciously think this thought over and over. I make this part of my daily routine.

I am always finding old beliefs and thought patterns that I'd never paid attention to or never knew were there. As soon as I find them, I snatch them up like weeds and begin this process again; first, creating a new belief, and then verbally killing the old one, while consciously thinking the new belief over and over until it becomes my subconscious truth.

I am often asked how I know when the thought has "stuck," how do I know it's my truth. I always reply with, "You'll know." Often, it's when you hear someone else say or maybe even hear on television, the original belief. Instantly, it catches your attention and you think, "That's not true." This has happened every time I consciously worked on this. My assistant asked me a few months ago, if I thought the universe was sending signs, and while that could be it, I lean more toward the thought process that now that you have a new belief, you can clearly hear the ones that are nonsense.

Next, you have to realize you can't create these beliefs by simply listing what you desire and leaving it there. Daily, you have to consciously spend time in this success place until unconsciously you're there 24/7. This means time carved out every day to repeat the new beliefs. Time spent thinking and seeing yourself as successful. Remember when I said be really specific about what you desire? It's the same way when you begin to visualize and see yourself. Be as specific as possible with what you see. Really put yourself in that success place. What do you look like? How do you dress? What do you drive? Or is someone else driving you? Do you have a chef? A housekeeper? What does your home look like? How does it feel to walk through it? Can you see the floorplan? Let's look deeper at your business. What does it look like? Do you have employees? If so, how many? Are you working out of your home or do you have outside offices? Who are the dream clients/customers with whom you are working? What makes them a dream to work with?

Really get into your vision. It takes practice, but soon, you'll be doing this with ease.

Even today, as my vision has grown bigger, I do this practice. For a minimum of 30 minutes a day, I am "seeing" myself where I desire to be. Sometimes, I do 30 minutes at once. Sometimes, I break it up into several visualization sessions a day, and, sometimes, I do more. Any free time I have I spend doing this on top of the 30 minutes I carve out.

It is important you realize that this practice, while keeping the same circle, will do zero good. Nothing much will change. You'll work on yourself internally, and then go back into the same circle of people telling you the original thought you're working to eradicate.

I remember when I was first beginning to go through this process. I tried to keep connections with friends as much as possible, but I felt like a mouse on a wheel. I spent about six months limiting my conversations with people outside of my household. If we were to go even deeper, I actually limited conversation with those in my household as well. I wouldn't spend more than 30 minutes a week talking to anyone who had a thought process similar to the one I was working to rid myself of. Sure, people thought I wasn't being a friend and their feelings were hurt, but I chose to put me first. And I simply wasn't strong enough to go into a room full of negativity. My light wasn't quite bright enough to drown out the darkness.

I compare it to someone addicted to drugs. If you're in an outpatient rehab facility, you may go into rehab for an hour or two a day. When you go home, you can't go back to the same surroundings that helped create the addiction in the first place. Your drug-addicted friends must go. It's not that you don't love them, but you love you and your sobriety more.

I also think it is worth noting that in addition to my visualizations and mantras around my new beliefs, I spent at least an hour a day reading books about mindset and wealth. When I wasn't reading, I had an audiobook playing in the background. I swear, my then four year old, knew many of the words to Florence Scovel Shinn's *The Game of Life and How to Play it*, which is a book I highly suggest if you're new to this mindset work. I continue to go back to this book, from time to time. It will always be one of my favorites, as I listened to it or read it every day, for two years.

This work isn't something that happens in one day, one week or even a month. The changes take place over a period of time, often with you not consciously noticing. Signs are your finances becoming consistently better or business seeming to come to you with more ease than previously.

I started this work in 2011. I began to notice differences within about a month, but it wasn't until 2014 I noticed the biggest difference outside of the massive growth of my business. Despite the growth my business had seen, I remained somewhat money conscious. Whenever I'd go into a store, I was sure to check prices. Although, I knew the money was in the account, I'd gone years worried that one day I'd scan the card at checkout and be declined, so I watched my money to a "T," even when I knew I had more than enough. It had become ingrained in me.

In the winter of 2014, while in Malta, I went to a local mall to pick up more winter clothes for my son and me. After walking though the department store and proceeding to the register, as I'm being rung up, I realized something huge. I hadn't checked the price on anything. I had breezed through the entire store picking up what we needed with the full-abundance mindset that what I needed was there. Tears began to stream down my face. I am aware that this may seem small to some, but this was like the final cord of lack being cut. I'd seen massive business growth; I was traveling all over the world; I'd built my team and I was happy as ever, but a little voice inside always had me a bit worried about that "decline." Yet, here I stood, for the first time in my adult life, and this wasn't a thought. Three years of daily work, 1,095 days of visualizing, mantras and studying, and the cord had been cut. This was huge, and a moment I will always remember, as it signifies so much.

So, understand that *this* is great work. Work that holds the key to you completely changing, not just your business, but your life. The 80 percent truly is a complete game changer, if you have the tenacity to follow through and do the work.

Reading List

Over the last few years, I have found a handful of mindset books that will help change the way you think about life, money and what is possible. Remember, we become what we spend the most time thinking about, so consciously spend your time reading and studying materials that will get you where you desire, as opposed to where you don't want to go.

1. *The Game of Life and How to Play It* by Florence Scovel Shinn
2. *The Science of Getting Rich* by Wallace D Wattles
3. *The Power of I AM and the Law of Attraction* by RJ Banks
4. *The Genie Within: Your Subconscious Mind and How to Use It* by Harry Carpenter
5. *Think and Grow Rich* by Napoleon Hill
6. *Leveraging the Universe and Engaging the Magic* by Mike Dooley
7. *The Law of Divine Compensation: On Work, Money, and Miracles* by Marianne Williamson
8. *The Source of Miracles* by Kathleen McGowan
9. *The Alchemist* by Paulo Coelho
10. *Money, and the Law of Attraction* by Esther and Jerry Hicks

The 20 Percent

"Anyone can take action. The one who succeeds will take inspired action."

The action. Many people take action for the sake of taking action, truly not knowing what to do on a day-to-day basis within their business. It is no wonder, though. Most have no idea what goal they are reaching toward or they are reaching toward so many at one time that the mind is divided and has no idea what action to take.

This is not a problem for those that follow the 80/20 rule of success.

Something amazing happens when you follow the 80 percent. You begin to operate with a clear mind. There is no divide, and there is no sense of overwhelm or confusion. The anxiety that often is talked about dissipates. All energy is being focused in one direction and the 20 percent begins to take care of itself.

I am often asked how I am able to remain as focused as I am. It is quite simple. I follow the 80 percent. I focus specifically on what I want. I see myself with it, and I think about what a project is going to look like when it is finished. I keep my eyes focused on the prize. Because I consistently do the work to rid myself of beliefs and thought patterns that no longer serve me, I am not having to deal with the fear that once upon a time would come up for me. And when I do experience fear, it's not paralyzing. It is fear that I am able to move through.

With the 80 percent handled, I wake up every morning clear about my goal. If anything comes up that doesn't lead to the goal that I have in mind, I don't do it. I wake up excited to take inspired action and work toward my goal.

A tool that I have used often through the years and that many of my clients use is my Productivity Planner and Goal Book. It's a full-year business planner focused specifically on keeping you productive. I created it specifically for the 20 percent, and it only works if you've done the 80 percent work.

I can't tell you how great it has been having something like this. I wake up every morning knowing the goal. I open the planner and, at a glance, see precisely what to do for the day. I choose what fits the goal I set in the 80 percent, and I take the action. Because there is no divided mind, I take the action with massive confidence to full execution.

But remember, your action will be half-assed if you haven't done the 80 percent work, if you haven't taken the time to do what requires the *real* effort.

Here's what I believe:

1. You were put on this earth to do big, amazing things.
2. Deep down you knew that already.
3. When you realize that you are truly worthy of all that this Universe has for you, you'll step up, go out and get it.
4. You are ready, now, to say yes to yourself, and what you desire.
5. Nothing's going to stop you but you.

Final Thoughts

I've been in this industry for many years. I've seen many people come and go. A lot of those businesses that fell by the wayside were good—often really good. The problem wasn't their work; the problem was they spent too much time in the hustle phase and not enough time looking at the things that were holding them back.

I have this theory that when you are a person brought to this earth to help facilitate transformation and, for whatever reason, you give up or are forced to shut your doors, you've not only let you down, you've let down the thousands of people you were put on this earth to help. Who will they turn to who does what you do in the way that you do it? It is your duty to truly get in line with what it takes to be successful. It is your duty to not only take the action but use the effort that the masses refuse to use.

I assume that if you've gotten to this point, you realize you aren't one of the masses. You don't fit into a neat little box with a ribbon on top. You have a message that needs to be told from the highest height. You know this deep down but, for some reason, you've been unable to grab on to what is needed to get your message out in a bigger way. I know a way. Are you ready? If you are, commit to Shutting up and Doing the Work— the work that you were put on this earth to do. Let's Go!

My free gift to you

As a thank you for investing in yourself, I am gifting you two tickets to a Shut Up and Do the Work live workshop in a city near you.

This workshop takes this book to the next level helping you dive even deeper into what is holding you back from accomplishing the things you desire to accomplish and then removing those blocks.

Visit www.ShutUpAndDoTheWork.com/Workshop for more information and to claim your tickets.

53852194R00055

Made in the USA
Lexington, KY
22 July 2016